This book has been published in cooperation with Evans Publishing Group.

Published in the United States by
Amicus
P.O. Box 1329, Mankato, Minnesota 56002

Printed in China by New Era Printing Co.Ltd

Library of Congress Cataloging-in-Publication Data
Rooney, Anne.
  Creative and media careers / by Anne Rooney.
     p. cm. -- (In the workplace)
  Summary: "Describes jobs in the creative and media sectors. Includes information on actors,
  sound engineers, journalists, designers, and more, covering their responsibilities and training
  needed. Also includes profiles of workers in the industry"--Provided by publisher.
  Includes bibliographical references and index.
  ISBN 978-1-60753-090-9 (library binding)
  1. Arts--Vocational guidance--Juvenile literature. 2. Mass media--Vocational guidance--Juvenile literature. I.
Title.
  NX163.R66 2011
  700.23--dc22

                                                                          2009054194

Editor and picture researcher: Patience Coster
Designer: Guy Callaby

The author would like to thank the following for their help in producing this book: Quentin Cooper, BBC; Mark
Shillam, *The Times*; Bob Portal, Fidelity Films; Gillan McClure, illustrator; Fiona Parker, Royal Opera House.

We are grateful to the following for permission to reproduce photographs:
Alamy 22 (Eddie Gerald), 32 (Helene Rogers), 37 (Scott Hortop), 38 (Steve Atkins Photography); Corbis 8 (Mark
Peterson), 9 (Bobby Yip/Reuters), 10 (Gaetan Bally/Keystone), 11 (Erica Berger), 12 (George McNish/Star
Ledger), 13 (Rob Grabowski/Retna Ltd), 15 (Adam Woolfitt), 16 (Markus Moellenberg), 17 (Tony Roberts), 18
(Alex Hofford/epa), 19 (TWPhoto), 21 (Nir Elias/Reuters), 23 (Erica Berger), 24 (John Schults/Reuters), 25
(Chien-Min Chung), 26 (Brooks Kraft), 27 (Tomas Rodriguez), 28 (Tim Clayton), 29 (Georg Hochmuth/epa), 30
(Dustin Snipes/Icon SMI), 31 (Peter Steffen/epa), 35 (Alessandro Garofalo/Reuters), 39 (Alessandra Benedetti),
40 (TWPhoto), 41 (Louie Psihoyos/Science Faction), 42 (Kerry Hayes/Twentieth Century Fox/Bureau L.A.
Collection); Getty Images 6 (AFP), 7 (Marcus Lyon), cover and 33 (Zigy Kaluzny-Charles Thatcher), 34 (Alan
Levenson), 36 (Karen Moskowitz); Kobal Collection 14 (BBC Films/Focus Features), 20 (Columbia/Tri-Star/Zade
Rosenthal), 43 (Wayans Bros/Revolution Studios/Joseph Lederer).

05 10
PO1568

9 8 7 6 5 4 3 2 1

IN THE
WORKPLACE

Creative

AND *Media*

Careers

ANNE ROONEY

amicus
mankato, minnesota

Contents

Working in the Creative and Media Sector

Careers in the creative sector and the media—television, radio, journalism, and publishing—are varied and exciting. They range from running advertising campaigns to writing the news, from designing clothes to dancing. But it's not all glamour. It's hard work, too.

SUIT YOURSELF

It's important to choose a career that suits your personal strengths, interests, and personality. Think about your particular skills and character. Do you like to work in a team or alone? Are you a whiz with technology, good with words, or better working with your hands? You might have a burning desire to work in a particular field. If so, think about what you want to do in that area. If you want to work in films, think about whether you want to be on screen or whether you would rather write scripts, manage lighting, or design sets.

A host of creative professionals work to get every performance perfect on stage or screen.

FINDING A JOB
Creative and media jobs are advertised in national and local newspapers, online, and in special industry publications. You can find these in the library or a careers office. Look for internships with large organizations, and try to gain relevant work experience.

Behind the scenes, lighting, sound, and sets are all controlled using complex technology.

BEATING THE COMPETITION
Creative and media careers are exciting and enjoyable, so finding a job is very competitive. There is a lot you can do to give yourself the best chance. Start by learning as much as you can about the field you want to work in. That might mean watching lots of television or animated films; going to the theater, movies, or concerts; exploring different types of computer games; or studying fashion magazines. Or it may mean taking lots of photos, drawing, designing outfits, and making things. It sounds fun, but you need to look at the aspects of a field that you don't like as well as those you do, so that you find out everything about it.

GET INVOLVED
Try to build as much knowledge and experience as you can to prove to employers that you are serious about your career choice. Find out about the organizations working in the field, the current trends, and how the industry works. Read trade magazines and look online for resources and industry blogs. Take every chance you can to meet and talk to people who work in the area. The more you can learn, the better your chances of success. Consider volunteering or doing an internship; you will work for low pay or for free, but you will learn useful skills.

ON YOUR OWN
Many people working creatively are self-employed or freelance. They don't have a single employer and regular pay, but take on work for different clients. To do this, you need to be disciplined and organized. You also need to be able to manage money and cope with stress—with having too much work sometimes and not enough work at other times. Being self-employed is a rewarding way to work, and there is a lot of help and advice available.

TO WORK IN THE CREATIVE AND MEDIA SECTOR, YOU WILL NEED
•
creativity
•
imagination
•
enthusiasm and determination
•
the ability to handle constructive criticism

Center Stage

Being a performer—an actor, musician, dancer, or other performance artist—is one of the most thrilling creative careers. Many people who perform professionally have practiced since early childhood and have always known what they wanted to do. You must have talent, but there are many other qualities you need to achieve success.

ACTOR

An actor's job is to bring characters and stories to life. He or she may work on the stage, in films, on TV, or on radio. Projects that need actors range from big-budget movies and TV series to commercials and street performances. There is a big difference between performing live and giving a performance that is recorded in a studio and shown later. In a live performance, there is no chance to "do it over" if you make a mistake. Everyone has to carry on as well as possible if things go wrong. Many performers find this exhilarating and say that it gives their performance an edge.

FINDING A JOB
To find acting jobs, look in trade publications or online job listings. Get lots of practice working with amateur and youth theater groups. Professional training at drama school is excellent preparation; most working actors have this. Most actors are also members of an actors' union. This makes it easier to get work, and it offers some protection against bad working conditions and terms.

A director gives instructions to the cast of a stage play.

TO BECOME AN ACTOR, YOU WILL NEED
●
acting talent
●
the ability to work with others and follow direction
●
confidence performing in public
●
a "thick skin"—there will be many failed auditions among successes

BIG BUILDUP

What an audience sees (or hears) of an actor's work is just a small part of the process. As well as performing, actors have to rehearse parts, carry out research, and learn about the subject of their performance. Many actors also sing or dance, or both. They have to practice these skills, too. It is often hard physical work.

Some actors are part of a theater company or group and work with the same people most of the time. Others move from one project to another, having to form working relationships quickly with new production staff and other performers. Actors often have some scope to interpret a role and bring something of their own to it. Even so, actors generally work under a director who has clear ideas about how the whole production should turn out. Each actor must follow the guidance of the director and work cooperatively with other members of the cast and production team.

NOT JUST STAGE AND SCREEN

As well as high-profile work—such as appearing on stage and in films or TV shows—many actors work in smaller venues and on smaller projects, at least while they are building up their careers.

If you want to be an actor, you may start off by working at publicity events and festivals, working at resorts, visiting schools or prisons, and perhaps even working on cruise ships. Most actors are self-employed and are paid a fee for each performance or contract. Successful actors often have an agent to represent them and negotiate contracts for work.

Many actors start out in unusual roles, perhaps in commercials or theme parks.

A radio announcer must be comfortable with the technology of the studio, including recording equipment and a teleprompter.

ANNOUNCER

An announcer works on TV or radio, talking to a camera or into a microphone. Announcers are the glue that holds a program together—they host a show, introduce stories, interview guests and experts, explain a topic, and mediate between different guests discussing a subject. An announcer might be on air for only a few hours a week, but he or she needs to do a huge amount of preparation. Many announcers research and edit their own material. It takes many hours of preparation to produce even a short TV or radio show.

GETTING READY

An announcer may work with the rest of the production team to decide the topic and various stories to be covered in the show. He or she will then need to research the topic, prepare or help to prepare a script, and prerecord any interviews or reports that will be dropped in. The work may involve traveling to film or record in another location. The announcer works with sound and video technicians, camera operators, and other production and directing staff. For television programs, there will also be wardrobe and makeup professionals working to prepare the announcer for the studio lights and camera.

MAIN TASKS:
TV OR RADIO ANNOUNCER

●

thinking of ideas for programs

●

researching stories and finding sources and interviewees

●

writing scripts

●

prerecording segments and interviews, perhaps editing them

●

speaking into the camera or microphone, working from a script or responding to other participants

Many announcers now edit their own work, especially those who work for smaller radio or TV stations. This means they need skills in sound and video editing, together with computer skills and confidence using technology. Editing involves removing passages that will not be used, splicing together the parts that will be used without leaving obvious breaks, and adding in any extra graphics (such as still photographs or animations).

KNOWING THE SUBJECT

Many announcers work in a particular area. They might present sports programs, political commentaries, an arts show, or a music program. They have special knowledge in that area and may have trained first in their specialty and only later moved into broadcasting. Others present more general material, such as a local news show. They still need research skills so that they can quickly get up to speed on any topic they have to cover.

ON AIR

For a live broadcast, the announcer may work from a script or teleprompter but may also have to respond to what other participants say or do. The announcer introduces prerecorded segments, interviews guests, provides links between items in the show, and may present his or her own material.

TO BECOME A TV OR RADIO ANNOUNCER, YOU WILL NEED

●

excellent presentation skills

●

journalism and communication skills

●

a good voice

●

the ability to stay calm under pressure

The host of a TV show greets guests and puts them at ease before the broadcast.

An announcer on a live radio show must be confident and spontaneous.

Quentin: Radio Announcer

"While studying science [in college], I became involved in the student film society. I particularly enjoyed the media and publicity side, so this swayed me into journalism. I started in print journalism with a little radio work, then [switched to the study of journalism]. When I finished, I became a trainee [with a major news network]. I came up with ideas for lively arts and youth programs, which I was allowed to make.

"I began producing arts programs for a radio [station], and while I was working as [an announcer], my sordid past in science was discovered. I was offered science and technology programs to present, ending with a long-running [radio show].

"I work freelance, and I'm very happy with where I am now. Every day is different, although there's a lot of sitting in front of a computer researching or writing. Each week I introduce people on the show who know much more about a subject than I do, so I have to do a lot of background work. Apart from writing a script and thinking up questions, I see my job as keeping the conversation flowing, directed, and still anchored to the [general audience]. I want everyone listening to get something from the show. Sometimes I succeed, sometimes I don't."

MUSICIAN

Musicians, dancers, and other performance artists use a skill they have been learning and practicing for many years. They don't all have formal training, though many do, but they do all have talent and the determination to succeed in a very competitive career. Musicians range from pop singers to instrumentalists in orchestras. The variety of music, instruments, and venues for performance is huge. What all professional musicians have in common is a love of music, natural talent, and the willingness to put in a lot of work practicing, rehearsing, performing, and finding work. Some musicians play live at music venues, others record music in a studio, and many do both.

DAY TO DAY

Every musician or singer needs to practice daily. You will already be doing this if you want to be a professional musician. Once you are working, you will also need to rehearse, usually with other performers. You may need to spend time looking for or writing new music and learning it. If you play an instrument, you will need to maintain it and arrange for safe transportation when going to performances.

Musicians, even if they perform solo, do not work alone. They need to deal with agents, with staff organizing musical events, and with recording or broadcast studios. Musicians also need to know the technical aspects of how sound travels in an auditorium or recording studio and how to work with the technologies used for recording and amplifying sound. Often, musicians have to work demanding hours, with performances during evenings and weekends. They need stamina and to be physically fit and healthy to put up with the rigors of traveling, performing, and working long hours.

HANDY HINT
Musicians often make extra money playing at parties, at other private events, or in bars. Some record music and post it on the Internet for free downloading to help build up a fan base.

It looks like fun, but a career as a musician takes stamina and hard work.

Behind the Scenes

It takes many more people than just the performers to make a successful broadcast, film, or performance. The supporting staff behind the scenes are just as important. They organize and shape the production, provide costumes and sets, and handle the complex technology used for sound and video.

SET DESIGNER

A set designer works to provide and prepare all the props (objects) that are needed for a film, video production, or stage play. The set designer follows the directions of the production design team to buy or make props so that they fit the period, design, and other requirements of the production. Set designers may find themselves hunting for a 1940s telephone one day and producing a Roman villa or the interior of an alien spaceship the next.

INDOORS AND OUTDOORS

Set designers prepare a set before filming or a performance starts, but they may also be called on during the production to ensure continuity or make changes. Many sets are made in a studio or on a stage, but some are created on location: out of the studio, in the open air, or in another building. Many TV programs and commercials are filmed in real houses, and the set designer then needs to work with the owner's personal possessions and decor. This takes tact and care.

TO BECOME A SET DESIGNER, YOU WILL NEED

●

a good eye for design

●

knowledge of modern and antique furniture and other objects

●

the ability to follow instructions

A historical production such as The Other Boleyn Girl *must be meticulously researched.*

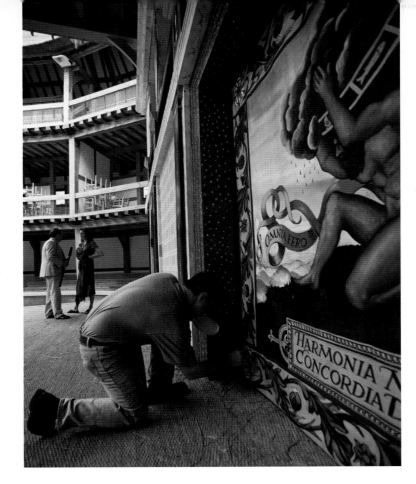

Skills from carpentry to painting are needed to prepare a stage set.

MAKING ROOMS

As a set designer, you will need a good knowledge of design and interior decorating, furniture and furnishings, how colors work together, and the properties of textiles and other materials. The work often involves researching a historic period or a particular look in order to recreate a scene convincingly. You will need to know about or be able to research special crafts that may be involved in producing props—these could range from glass-blowing to taxidermy. You will deal with some delicate and valuable objects, and heavy items, so you'll need to know how to handle them safely and securely, following health and safety regulations.

FITTING TOGETHER

Set designers need to use computers with graphic design software and understand scale drawings and plans so that they can place objects accurately on the set. They need to know how their work fits into the process of producing a film or live production.

There are opportunities for set designers to work on feature films, television programs, commercials, music videos, and stage productions such as plays, operas, and musicals.

MAIN TASKS:
SET DESIGNER
•

sourcing and preparing objects and furnishings; following instructions but also making independent decisions quickly when necessary

•

dealing with craftspeople, designers, and others involved in making props to ensure a correct and consistent look

•

interpreting and following detailed scale plans of a set, and using planning and design software

•

redesigning the set quickly during the production or filming

•

dealing politely with members of the public when filming on location or in private homes

SOUND ENGINEER

A sound engineer works to get the best possible sound quality in recorded and live broadcasts and recordings. Many sound engineers work in the music industry, supporting bands on stage and making recordings in the studio. Films, TV and radio programs, commercials, corporate videos, and all kinds of stage productions also need sound engineers. Even video games and web sites often use sound effects, music, or speech. Some sound engineers work in the music technology industry, helping with new developments in, for example, hi-fi systems and recording equipment.

Sound engineers often have to produce good-quality sound in difficult circumstances—interviews with strikers on a noisy picket line or a band playing at an outdoor music festival, for example. The work involves using sophisticated computerized audio equipment, including microphones, amplifiers, sound-mixing desks, and sound-enhancing software. A good knowledge of physics, electronics, sound technology, and math is essential.

HANDY HINT
If you are interested in becoming a sound engineer, start by gaining experience and learning the basics through volunteering with a small community radio station or working as a DJ. Look into journalism or theater classes in sound production. These may be offered by a college or tech school.

CLEAN SOUNDS

Working with music, sound engineers have to record each instrument to a separate track and combine the tracks to produce a perfect sound. A sound engineer has to balance volume; clean up recordings to remove background noise, hiss, and interference; cut out bits that are not needed; and splice together sections of a recording so that the piece sounds continuous. As a sound engineer, you will have to keep careful records and logs so that the source of any piece of sound can be identified and nothing is lost.

It can take a long time to make a perfect recording. The performer and sound engineers must be patient and committed.

LIVE AND KICKING

To work as a sound engineer, you need a "good ear" and excellent hearing. A wide knowledge of musical styles is necessary, too, if you want to work with music, as you will need to know what listeners and performers are hoping for from your work. The aim is to make it sound as though the listener is actually present, hearing the sound live.

Recording sports programs for television or radio in the open air can be a real challenge.

Matt: Sound Engineer

"In my teens, I used to build sound systems and do some DJ-ing; I had a passion for music and was fascinated by sound in a rather geeky way. I went to gigs and concerts, and I'd often ask if I could check out the [equipment]. I'm not sure how many bands would allow that now.

"I trained in electronics and got a job in [an audio] company working on speaker design. My job now is in sound quality, and I spend a lot of time in a soundproof and anechoic chamber (anechoic means the walls absorb all sound) with my eyes closed, listening to music! I use lots of electronic equipment to measure sound quality, including lasers, but the human ear is still the best gauge. There are elements of sound that we can hear but we can't measure yet, and some of the words I use to describe sound don't sound very technical, but here we all know what they mean."

Video editors have to work quickly and confidently to produce a breaking news story.

VIDEO EDITOR

A video editor works from raw footage to put together a piece of film that can be shown, broadcast, or put on a web site. Video editors may work on films, TV programs, commercials, corporate and training videos, video games, and web sites.

Video editing is a post-production process carried out on a computer. The editor transfers film or video footage to the computer and then chooses the parts to use, cuts them out, and splices them together in order. The editor has to match the video to sound, which may be speech, music, or sound effects, and make sure they are synchronized. The first full version is called a "rough cut." It is reviewed by other people involved in the production, and the video editor then takes their feedback and suggestions and makes any necessary changes to refine and complete the project. This involves using software to enhance images, adding title sequences, a soundtrack, captions, and special effects. The video editor prepares the package for final presentation for delivery, usually as a DVD.

MAIN TASKS:
VIDEO EDITOR

●

moving footage to computer from cameras, film, video, and archives

●

selecting and cutting shots, splicing them together into a sequence as a rough cut, following directions and using initiative, and sometimes working to a script

●

working cooperatively with camera operators, sound engineers, directors, producers, and other members of the production team to get the required result

●

adding and "syncing" sound (music, voice, sound effects)

●

using software to enhance shots digitally and add special effects; adding graphic effects, titles, and captions

WHERE WILL I BE?

Work experience or an internship in a small production company or community radio or TV station is a good way to get vital early experience. Many editors first take a job as a runner in a production company, using the opportunity to learn as much as possible about the industry. Your next step may be to work as a digitizer, converting film or tape to a digital format that can be edited on computer. As assistant editor, you will help the senior video or sound editor and learn the details of the job. After this, you will be ready for a job as a video or sound editor in your own right.

PRACTICE SHOTS

If you want to work as a video editor, you should find out as much as you can about the process of filming. You should also experiment—use a digital video camera or animation software to make your own "shorts," adding sound effects and titles to create a finished production. There are many places where you can upload and showcase your work on the web, building your own portfolio of films. You should also try to gain experience using professional equipment. You may be able to do this working on school or community productions.

Director Andrew Adamson looks at the rough edit of the film Prince Caspian *with a video editor.*

TO BECOME A PRODUCER, YOU WILL NEED

●

organizational ability

●

an excellent network of contacts

●

skills in managing people

PRODUCER

A producer may work in film, television, radio, or live performance (theater or opera, for example). He or she is in charge of the whole show. It's the producer who comes up with the idea for a production and sees it right through to the finished performance. At the start of a project, a producer develops an idea so that it can be shown to investors and participants, including cast and crew. Next, the producer may commission someone to write a script, or buy the rights to use an existing script or book. Often, the producer is also the director and has a hands-on role in directing film shoots or recording, choosing locations, managing script writers, and so on. The smaller the scale of the project, the more the producer has to do at each stage.

ON THE ROAD

The producer of a live production may have to organize a tour, choosing locations and venues and organizing the transportation of people, equipment, and sets. He or she may also arrange the recruitment of local staff. The same issues face a producer of a film or program being made on location.

MASTERING TECHNOLOGY

Although producers may not do any recording or editing themselves, they must keep up-to-date with the technologies used for sound and video recording, editing, and broadcasting so that they know exactly what is possible. Increasingly, producers need to understand new methods of delivery, too: Their work may be delivered using the web, cell phones, or media players such as the iPod.

Director Tim Burton (right) on the set of Big Fish *with the movie's producer Richard Zanuck.*

Producer Peter Ho-Sun Chan gives directions to an actress on the set of the film Bodyguards and Assassins.

Bob: Film Producer

"I had no connections in the film industry, though I ran the university film society as a student, so I wrote to every film-related company asking for a job. I took the only offer, working as a runner at a post-production house, and I worked my way through a series of positions.

"I won a producer's [position] at [an arts school for] film and television on the strength of a short film that had played at festivals. After [that], I worked line-producing low-budget features and producing music videos. Eventually, I started a production company with a German producer. We developed and produced our own features and worked on large co-productions. Later I started Fidelity Films, which develops and produces features for the international market.

"A film goes through development, production, and post-production. In development, I research scripts and locations, develop ideas with writers and directors, raise [money, hire] cast and deal with agents, create schedules and budgets, and generally put the project together. During production I'm managing the shoot, then handling post-production to deliver a quality film to the investors and distributors who have paid for it. I can work 12 hours a day or more as the film is shot and then post-produced. Producers only make money once a movie is in production. Even the most successful film producers often have unexpected career lulls. As they say in Hollywood, you're only as good as your last picture!"

Words and Pictures

Many people think first of journalism when considering creative and media jobs. Journalism is a large field that offers careers in different media. There are many other jobs working with words, including editing, and more jobs for photographers and artists or illustrators.

JOURNALIST

Journalists write articles on news, topical subjects, or areas of general interest. They may work in print, writing for newspapers, magazines, and corporate newsletters, or they may be broadcast journalists, working in radio or TV. More and more journalists also write for web sites and blogs; this demands its own special skills, including an understanding of how web pages are put together.

To work as a journalist, you will need to have excellent writing skills and an "eye" for a good story—the ability to spot something that will interest an audience. Broadcast journalists have to prepare scripts, so writing is still important, but they also need presentation skills, speaking clearly and fluently to the camera

Journalists sometimes have to work in dangerous situations, such as this conflict zone in the country of Georgia.

A news anchor meets with his team to discuss news coverage.

or microphone. A news journalist must remain confident and calm even in difficult circumstances. Sometimes, newsgathering and reporting can be dangerous or distressing—working in a war zone or covering a natural disaster is not for the faint-hearted. It's important to be able to work quickly and to meet deadlines, as journalism runs on very tight schedules —there's no chance to be an hour late with a radio or TV news bulletin.

NOT JUST NEWS

Many journalists, even if they come to work on national and international news later, begin by covering small events and court cases for local media and gradually move toward more time-critical news work. Not all journalists cover breaking news. Some specialize in areas such as sports, music, business, travel, technology, arts, or legal matters.

Many journalists spend time researching and investigating a story, interviewing experts or witnesses, and then putting together an in-depth story. They need good research skills and the ability to communicate well with others, encouraging them to open up and share information.

GETTING STARTED

There are plenty of journalism and media courses, but many publications and broadcasters are happy to take trainees with expertise or training in another area. To get your work into print, try offering articles to specialty magazines on a topic you know about (perhaps a hobby), or write for local free papers or magazines to help you to build a portfolio. Some journalists start with a staff job at a local newspaper, but many others work freelance for their whole career.

HANDY HINT
The Internet gives you plenty of chances to write for an audience and build your skills. Try starting a blog on a topic you know about; it can act like an online showcase that potential employers may look through to see evidence of your writing skill.

The editorial staff decide which stories to run and how to present them.

Mark: Deputy Editor

"After a [college degree] in journalism, I got my first reporting job on a local newspaper. I moved to a regional evening newspaper as news editor and then assistant editor before starting as a [political] editor on a national paper. I was chief [political editor] before becoming deputy editor.

"I'm responsible for the content and production of the main inside news pages every day, covering local news, foreign news, financial news, and (occasionally) sports. I work with the [department editors], newsdesk, photo desk, designers, and editor-in-chief to make sure the pages come together as intended. I make sure we get the right stories in the right places with the right [photos] and the right headlines. You have to be able to get up to speed on any subject very quickly and assess news value instantly.

"A typical day can start with a morning conference. Then I'll start work on a news framework and any special layout. At an afternoon conference, we thrash out what's going where. Then I work with the designers and sort out pictures, while agreeing with the news editors on the content and length of the stories. The pages are put together as the copy comes in. There are lots of last-minute changes as new stories break or the editor and deputy change their minds about things before the first edition pages are sent off."

EDITOR

An editor works with writers to produce the final wording for books, magazines, newspapers, commercials, web sites, and corporate documents. There are also editors working in TV, radio, and film.

There are many different types of editorial work, but all editors need excellent language skills and an eye for detail. They need to be able to work confidently and cooperatively with others, and to be both tactful and firm when dealing with writers. The editor has overall responsibility for the project and directs its creation, from commissioning the writers and illustrators or photographers to approving the final arrangement of text and images. An editor may make or supervise changes to text, perhaps restructuring it or asking for another chapter. Editors need management skills and good contacts, so that they can identify the best people to work on any particular project. They also need to know how to use the different types of computer software involved in writing and laying out a publication and working with photos and art.

WHERE WILL I BE?

Publishing is a competitive field. Many people start with an unpaid internship to gain work experience. A job as an editorial assistant may be the first rung on the ladder as you learn the basics of editing. As a copy editor, you clean up an author's text, cutting it to the right length and checking it. Experienced editors may move on to be managing or acquisitions editors, with responsibility for series of books and choosing new writers.

Staff on the Chinese edition of Vogue *discuss layouts for an issue of the magazine.*

PHOTOGRAPHER

A photographer may work on assignment, following direction from a client, or may approach publishers or potential clients with ideas. Most work freelance, but some are employed by newspapers, magazines, or studios. There is a wide range of work available, from covering the news to fashion, product, and portrait photography.

Press photographers working on the lawn of the White House in Washington, D.C., all trying to get the best shot.

SNAP HAPPY

Digital photography has made it much easier to practice taking photographs, but technical ability is still essential. Using cameras and lenses and understanding focus, lighting, and exposure are as important as they ever were. To work as a photographer, you'll need a good eye and creative flair to spot a good picture and compose a photo in a striking way. You'll use software to enhance photos and suit them to their particular purpose.

A NEW ROUTE

Traditionally, photographers begin their careers working for local press or in a studio, developing technical skills and learning techniques. Today, though, many follow a different route, putting photos online, selling them to stock photo agencies, and uploading them to news web sites. This is a good way of building a portfolio and finding an audience.

MAIN TASKS: PHOTOGRAPHER

●

discussing requirements with clients

●

planning and attending photo shoots or studio sessions

●

processing film and digital photographs; making prints or digital images

●

commercial negotiations with clients to sell work and further rights or licenses

ILLUSTRATOR

Illustrators produce illustrations for books, magazines, web sites, and promotional materials, or graphics for films or computer programs. They may use any medium, from pencils to computer software or embroidery. Most illustrators work to a specific assignment.

As an illustrator, you would use your artistic skill to interpret the client's specifications. After producing a plan or rough sketch, you would work with feedback from the client to develop the finished pieces. You may need to redo some pieces of art several times until you and the client are both satisfied.

An illustrator often works alone in a studio and may use traditional media or a computer.

Gillian: Picture Book Writer/Illustrator

"As a child, I earned money by making my relatives pay to read stories I'd written and illustrated! Now I write and illustrate children's books professionally.

"Writing and illustrating is a business as competitive as any other. It's important to understand the market and to work in partnership with publishers—not just the editors, but the foreign rights department, publicity, marketing, and sales.

"My working year follows the pattern of the publishers' year, dominated by the international book fairs. Within this is the rhythm of creating a book. First comes the writing stage—often away from my desk working on Post-it notes in a blank "dummy" book. Then I prepare rough illustrations, working closely with a designer and [typesetter]. Finally, I move into my painting studio to complete the artwork in color. But I also have to make time to prepare new projects to sell to publishers and for conference talks, workshops, committees, exhibitions of artwork, and visits to schools and libraries.

"I've never regretted choosing this career. I've had to cope with poverty, rejection, and working in isolation, but the reward of the completed book outweighs all these."

Making It Happen

Performers and producers can put together the best show in the world, but without promotion, no one will come to see it. As important as organizing an event is making the potential audience aware it is happening. Public relations, advertising, and promotion professionals all work to bring customers to performances and products.

EVENTS MANAGER

An events manager works with venues, artists, promoters, and backers to organize corporate, social, and promotional events. The event may be anything from a music festival to a product launch. Some events managers specialize in particular types of events, such as weddings or charity galas. Organizing a successful event depends greatly on contacts—on knowing who to call on for particular tasks—so an events organizer needs to be good at networking and maintaining a list of contacts.

Some events managers work within a venue, such as a hotel or theme park, putting together celebrations for a variety of clients. Others work in large organizations that arrange their own events, and still others work independently or for a business that specializes in organizing events for clients.

Events organizers deal with a huge range of different events and spectacles.

A huge ball is put together by an army of events organizers.

MAIN TASKS: EVENTS MANAGER

●

discussing requirements with clients and suggesting ideas for events

●

agreeing on budgets and schedules and working within them

●

researching and contracting venues, caterers, security, entertainers, and other suppliers

●

negotiating costs

●

handling invitations, promotion, advertising, and publicity

●

organizing insurance and contingency (backup) plans

●

overseeing an event as it happens, and dealing with any problems that arise

●

making sure everything is dismantled and cleared away and that everyone is paid following an event

HAVING A BALL

To be an events manager, you will need good communications skills, "people skills," organizational ability, and project management skills. Making a memorable event is a creative skill; it takes vision and imagination, the inspiration to generate new ideas, and the confidence to carry them through to fruition. An event brings together many people in different roles. You will need to keep an overview of the whole event while dealing with details and individual team members—it's like juggling; you need to keep all the balls in the air no matter the pressures and setbacks. As the organizer, it will be your job to keep everyone motivated, working within the budget, and on time. An event, once planned, is not movable, so you need to be able to stick to a very rigid deadline and reorganize any elements that run into difficulties.

FINDING A JOB

An education in events management may help you find a job in this area. Joining a professional organization may also lead to opportunities. Many people move into events management from helping to organize events in another role—perhaps working as a personal assistant and helping to plan conferences and corporate parties, for instance.

Advertising executives suggest the right form for an advertising campaign—it could be giant billboards at a sports venue.

ADVERTISING ACCOUNT EXECUTIVE

There are so many businesses trying to attract customers that huge amounts of money are poured into advertising to bring products, services, and events to the attention of people who may want them. An advertising account executive helps to put together the right advertising and promotional campaign to make a product or service stand out and catch the eye of customers.

The advertising account executive acts as a go-between for the advertising agency and the client—the company with something to sell. Account executives discuss with clients their needs and goals for advertising, then come up with exciting ideas for a strong campaign. It takes a mixture of creative, lateral thinking and a clear understanding of each client's business to offer good ideas. The next step is pitching ideas to the client. Pitching involves describing an idea persuasively so that the client can envision the campaign and its impact and decide whether it is what they want. It is a creative and dynamic job.

TO BECOME AN ADVERTISING EXECUTIVE, YOU WILL NEED

●

creativity, inspiration, and vision

●

excellent communication skills, in both writing and speaking

●

to be dynamic, persuasive, and hardworking

●

good business and negotiating skills

DYNAMIC CREATIVES

If you work as an advertising executive, you will need imagination and vision to think up original ideas. You will also need determination and organizational skills to work with designers and copywriters to turn your ideas into a successful advertising campaign. You must be quick thinking, have a good commercial sense, and be able to work within a budget and to strict deadlines.

Account executives often handle three or four contracts at the same time, developing advertising campaigns for different products or clients. These will be noncompeting products or services, so you may be handling, for instance, an account for a newspaper, another for a music distributor, and one for a breakfast cereal. You will need to manage and motivate a team within the agency, communicating your vision so that the writers and designers produce what you and the client want. An understanding of marketing and how advertising works to persuade people to buy things is vital.

WHERE WILL I BE?

Many advertising executives begin their careers by working as an administrative assistant in an advertising agency, rising to the level of junior account executive and learning on the job. It is also possible to start as a copywriter and move up to account manager. Some people transfer to advertising after working in PR (public relations) inside a large organization or at a PR agency.

SILVERY TONGUE

Advertising executives need extremely good communication and presentation skills. The work involves much face-to-face discussion and negotiation with clients. It's necessary to be persuasive, enthusiastic, and articulate to represent the agency and persuade clients to run with an idea.

Sometimes a campaign involves making models or computer graphics.

GRAPHIC DESIGNER

A graphic designer works with visual imagery to communicate ideas. Designers use pictures, photographs, typography, and layout to create an "identity" for an organization or to project a particular image. They may work on products, packaging, magazines, or advertising and may be asked for input into television advertising, web pages, or any other medium that tries to make a visual impact. Designers may work in a design studio, an advertising agency, or in the design department of a large organization.

GETTING THE LOOK

A graphic designer must have good visual and creative skills, an eye for design, and fine attention to detail. If you want to work as a graphic designer, you will need to know about art and design history and understand a number of different artistic methods and styles. You should look critically at all the designs you see around you in everyday life and try to figure out what works and why it has the impact it does.

A graphic designer often works on computer to combine text and graphic elements such as drawings, photographs, lines, and blocks of color to create a distinctive "look." The designer needs to know how to achieve different styles—how to make a design that looks comfortable and reassuring, or luxurious and indulgent, or edgy and exciting, for instance.

**MAIN TASKS:
GRAPHIC DESIGNER**

●

talking with clients or managers to decide requirements for a project

●

researching a project and the required look or image to be promoted

●

drawing up ideas as sketches or rough work

●

presenting ideas for discussion with others

●

responding to feedback and executing selected ideas, sometimes working with copywriters, illustrators, and photographers

A designer sketching an advertisement in a studio.

WORKING TOGETHER

Before starting a new project, the designer discusses what's needed with the client or manager. There may be particular colors, designs, pictures, or logos that have to be used because they are part of the client's corporate identity. The process of building a successful design involves many people, so the designer needs good communication skills and must respond positively to criticism and suggestions.

As a graphic designer, you may be asked to find or commission art or photographs, choose typefaces (text styles) for text, and choose a color scheme. To do this, you will need knowledge of photography, typeface design, how colors work together, and the psychology of how people respond to images, colors, and type styles.

Grace: Graphic Designer

"I began with a B.A. in graphic design before taking [an entry-level design job] in a small design agency. I have a few clients of my own now, and manage all their design projects, though I can call on help from other members of the agency if there's a large project I can't handle alone. We work together, bouncing ideas off each other a lot.

Graphic designers work closely with clients, so they need to be able to communicate their ideas effectively.

"There's not really any such thing as a typical day. I may spend the morning talking to a client, or at a meeting with the rest of the design team, or working at my drawing board or computer on a current design. At the moment, I'm working on packaging for a new range of products for one of my clients, and some posters and leaflets for a literary festival. The festival job involves working with a lot of text, which I don't usually do—I tend to specialize in graphics and typography. But it's an exciting challenge. I've also put together material for exhibition stands, designed brochures and [mailings], developed logos, and [established] corporate house styles."

Making Things

Many creative people like to make things, getting huge satisfaction from turning raw materials into beautiful or useful objects. If you want to make things with your hands, you might consider a craft such as pottery, glass-blowing, or furniture making. Or you may prefer to design objects that other people make.

PRODUCT DESIGNER

Product designers are responsible for the design of many everyday objects, from cell phones to saucepans. They make sure that products are easy, safe, and pleasant to use, look good, and are cost-effective to produce.

NICE THINGS

We live in an increasingly design-led world; there is so much choice for customers that design details are often the deciding factor in choosing one product over another. It is the product designer's task to come up with a product that customers will buy.

Product designers generally specialize in a particular area, such as consumer electronics, furniture, or cars; some work in very specialized areas, like medical technology. They may work in the design department of a large organization or in a design studio that deals with many clients.

MAIN TASKS:
PRODUCT DESIGNER
●
discussing plans with
the client
●
researching market
requirements, competing
products, materials,
and processes
●
coming up with ideas and
making sketches and notes
●
discussing the design and
models with the client
●
choosing materials
●
producing detailed drawings
and scale plans, complete with
costs, parts lists, and
specification of materials
●
making prototypes or models
of the product
●
correcting any problems with
the design and responding to
feedback and suggestions
●
testing the models, both
in real life and with
computer simulations

The design for a
new car is first
developed using
special computer
imaging software.

A product designer works from product specifications (specs), which include details of the product's function, how much it may cost, any particular features that are needed, and an idea of its place in the market—whether it is a luxury or economy item, for example. The designer prepares and presents initial ideas, responds to feedback, and makes mock-ups, models, or prototypes to show what the product will look like and how it will work. Designers must know about production processes so that they can judge realistically what can be manufactured.

MAKING IT REAL

To work as a product designer, you will need good graphics and design skills in order to produce detailed scale plans and drawings using computer design programs. You will also need a good understanding of materials and their properties so that you can choose suitable materials. Product designers must work well with others, accepting feedback on designs and cooperating with engineers, model-makers, and a marketing department. Although most product designers are based in a studio or design department, they may have to travel to visit factories where their products are made.

Innovative furniture design is a specialized branch of product design. This chair and footstool are part of a line by Italian designer Armani.

TO BECOME A PRODUCT DESIGNER, YOU WILL NEED

●

creative flair, with an ability to work in three dimensions

●

technical skills and knowledge

●

computer skills, to work with computer-aided design and modeling software

●

good communication, presentation, and teamwork skills

CLOTHING DESIGNER

A clothing designer may work in fashion or in costume for stage or screen. A fashion designer makes designs for clothes to sell anywhere from a ready-to-wear chain store to a haute couture house. Some designers specialize in particular items or types of clothing, such as shoes, men's clothes, or bridal wear. A designer working in costume designs the clothes worn for productions and events—anything from circus outfits to costumes for a historical drama or spacesuits for a sci-fi film.

CLOTHES FOR REAL LIFE

A fashion designer may work in mainstream fashion, ready-to-wear designer clothes, or high fashion (haute couture). Most designers work to specifications, but they need to bring their own vision and inspiration to their work and know about trends in fashion and where they are leading. As well as imagination, designers need technical skill and an understanding of how fabrics behave—clothes must perform well, not just look good.

A fashion designer adjusts a model's dress. Designers need to know how fabrics hang and what colors work best together.

TO BECOME A CLOTHING DESIGNER, YOU WILL NEED

•

flair, imagination, creativity

•

drawing skills

•

an eye for fashion and trends

•

excellent knowledge of fashion history and of textiles

FINDING A JOB
A degree in fashion, design, or textiles will improve your chances of finding a job. You will need a portfolio—a collection of your own designs—and to show that you can carry through a design and make the garment. Work experience in a design house will give you useful experience. Experience in fashion retail can help, too.

FROM DRAWING BOARD TO SHOP FLOOR

Designers sketch out designs and produce concept and "mood" boards, which bring together the colors, patterns, fabrics, and shapes that will create a themed collection. Knowledge of textiles and trim helps them to choose suitable materials for garments.

Often, a designer will work with machinists making up sample garments, though in a smaller design studio, designers may make up their own samples. Knowledge of textile-based crafts and skills such as sewing, knitting, tailoring, and pattern cutting is essential. Often, designers need to work within a budget and to price an item. They may need to travel to visit the factories making the clothes they have designed.

STAGE AND SCREEN

Designing costumes for performance requires additional skills. Many costumes are one-of-a-kind designs, so there is no need to research manufacturing processes, but the designer may also make the costume. Costume designers need an excellent knowledge of fashion history and clothes from around the world. They need to be able to research costumes worn in different periods, regions, and walks of life and recreate them using modern materials that will stand out during a performance.

Fiona: Assistant Costume Designer

"I've always been interested in working in theater, but it wasn't until I was [in college] that I discovered the job of a costume designer. My drama teacher helped me find a useful degree, a B.A. in stage design. It gave me vital skills, such as technical drawing, but also the experience of working on a real show.

A costume designer working on a costume for a stage production.

"It's a difficult career to get into, as [costume] designers work freelance, and most work comes from contacts. There are a few permanent jobs, such as resident/associate designer, with stage companies, but these generally go to well-known designers. You have to work unpaid when you are starting out, building up contacts and experience. I had a part-time job and worked my theater projects around it.

"I never do the same thing two days [in a row], and I'm always learning something new. In my first six months, I did a huge range of work, from designing and building small-scale fringe shows, to assisting costume supervisors on the musical Billy Elliot and model making for established designers. I can be fitting costumes one day, sourcing props the next and buying fabric the day after—all over the place. Although some days can be tough—the hours are very long and tiring—there's nothing like the feeling of getting it right and seeing your ideas come to life on stage."

CRAFTSPERSON

People who make a living from a craft very often work for themselves, though some may be part of a cooperative or larger workshop. Craftspeople often design the products they make, and also market or sell them, handle their own publicity, and buy the supplies they need.

Craftwork comes in many forms. This woman is making jewelry.

GOOD WITH YOUR HANDS

People make a living from a huge range of crafts, including pottery, woodcarving, ceramics, embroidery, and basketmaking. The first requirement is skill in your chosen craft. You will need to build a portfolio of examples or photos of your work to show if you want to be employed or win commissions from clients. Some craftspeople produce substantial pieces to commission; others produce a set of similar or identical items (perhaps necklaces or handmade shoes) and sell these to shops, at craft fairs, or on the Internet.

HANDY HINT
Go to craft fairs and markets to see what other people are selling and how much they charge. Ask local shops to sell some of your work. Many craftspeople sell their work online, often through sites such as eBay or Etsy.

This artist is making bronze sculptures in a workshop in Italy.

GOODS IN AND GOODS OUT

A craftsperson works with raw materials—anything from metal to wool—to make a finished product. Self-employed craftspeople must be good at controlling finances, negotiating with suppliers and banks, keeping detailed records of expenses, and calculating prices for their work. Many people start to build their craft business while employed, perhaps part-time.

LEARNING FROM EXPERTS

In some crafts, you can develop skills on your own. In others, training is useful, especially if you will be handling dangerous materials or equipment. No one could take up creative iron-working or glass-blowing on their own, as these are specialized skills and workers use dangerous equipment. If you want to go into a field like this, you will need to start as an assistant or apprentice in a workshop.

MAIN TASKS: CRAFTSPERSON

•

designing new products, perhaps to commission

•

researching and sourcing materials

•

making products

•

selling to shops or directly to customers

•

handling accounts, dealing with suppliers, marketing, negotiating with customers or sales outlets

Being Creative with Technology

Many creative professionals use high-tech equipment in their work, including design software, computerized video-editing programs, and sophisticated sound-recording equipment. Some jobs are carried out completely on a computer, such as making animations, doing web design, and building computer games. Special effects are created on a computer, or using robotics and other special equipment.

ANIMATOR

An animator produces animated films or sequences for commercials, TV, film, corporate videos, web sites, and games. There are many ways of making animations, including traditional drawing on paper, but many modern animated films and shorts are made mostly or entirely as computer graphics (CG).

Animators may work in two or three dimensions. Animations for web pages are often made using the design package Flash, which makes simple, smooth, 2D animations in solid colors. For complex CG animations, including feature films, animators design characters, scenery, and movement and then direct the action, instructing the computer to move the characters around the scenery, and recording the action. It takes a large team of programmers and animators and very powerful computer systems.

An animator working with a computer graphics program at a Tokyo film studio.

MAIN TASKS: ANIMATOR

●

following a storyboard to build animated sequences

●

working cooperatively with other animators and team members to build sequences into the whole production, ensuring continuity

●

using computers to produce images in an animation sequence (2D), or to define characters and their movements (3D)

●

checking and revising recorded animations

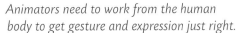

Animators need to work from the human body to get gesture and expression just right.

WHERE WILL I BE?
A degree in animation or computer science is a good starting point. Work experience as a runner in an animation studio is very valuable as it will give you an overview of the animation production process. The next step is to work as an animation assistant.

DRAWING AND ACTING

An animator has to bring characters to life, making them move realistically, and use motion, gesture, and expression to convey personality and emotion. This takes excellent artistic skills but also insight into how people respond and behave. If you want to work as an animator, acting classes or experience can be very useful, as they teach you how people use their bodies in these ways. Animators need a good feel for timing and movement, also skills used by successful actors.

ALL TOGETHER

The animated sequence is sketched out on a storyboard, and each animator is allocated one or more portions, or sometimes a character, which they animate throughout. It's necessary to work closely with other animators, with a director who determines the sequence, and with programmers and designers. Animators need a combination of computer skills and artistic ability.

SPECIAL EFFECTS TECHNICIAN

Blowing up a spaceship or sending an out-of-control robot on a killing spree in a crowded supermarket is all in a day's work for a special effects technician. The challenge for special effects is to make the unreal look real, whether it's an explosion, a gruesome injury, or an alien.

DICING WITH DEATH

Working on special effects involves producing the exciting and often dangerous sequences in films, TV, and commercials, or the special equipment used in stage shows. Special effects technicians usually have to work with large and complex machinery and often create pyrotechnic effects. They work with fire, dangerous chemicals, large machinery, robots, and fast-moving vehicles. This takes practical skills and knowledge of chemistry and physics to decide what will create the effect they want. A good knowledge and awareness of health and safety issues is essential, as is the ability to think and respond quickly if anything goes wrong.

MAKING THINGS TO DESTROY

Special effects technicians often have to make, or supervise the making of, the equipment that will be used, so technical skills are essential. They need to be confident using power tools and heavy machinery safely, but they also need imagination and creativity so that they can work out how to create the effect that is needed.

HANDY HINT
You can make a start by creating some special effects of your own and photographing or filming them to begin building a portfolio. Keep detailed notes of how you create each effect and how well it worked. You will be able to draw on these notes in later projects and gradually improve your skills.

The special effects that created Johnny Storm, the Human Torch, in the movie Fantastic Four *were added in post-production.*

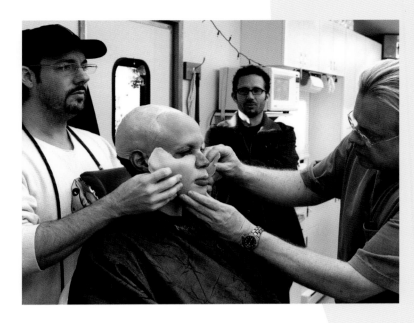

Special effects experts work on the face mask for an actor in the movie White Chicks.

GRUESOME AND FANTASTIC

Special effects work also covers producing prostheses, masks, and models to make actors look like monsters, to give them hideous fake wounds, or to change their appearance in other ways. Many masks and prostheses are made of rubber or acrylic, and are built using molds taken of the actor's own body. To create special effects with human, animal, or alien bodies, a knowledge of anatomy and how the body moves is useful.

WHO ARE YOU?

Whichever type of creative career you choose, you are likely to bring something of your own personality to your work. Reflecting on your character, your hopes and dreams, your beliefs, and your talent will help you to make a good choice. Think about how you like to work and what interests you. Because many creative careers demand a lot of personal and emotional investment, you will do best if you are wholly committed to and passionate about the line of work you have chosen.

BUILDING A PORTFOLIO

Most careers in the media and creative industries are very competitive. To give yourself a good chance, you will need a portfolio of work to showcase your skills and abilities. What goes into your portfolio depends on the type of career you want to follow. It may be full of drawings and illustrations, or of designs, photographs of things you have made, show reels, demo tapes, or articles you have published in print and online. Your portfolio is your record of achievement; you will continue to build it throughout your career, but it is never too early to start it.

TO BECOME A SPECIAL EFFECTS TECHNICIAN, YOU WILL NEED
●
practical skill in at least one area, such as pyrotechnics or model making
●
the ability to follow specs or a director's instructions
●
good awareness and knowledge of health and safety issues
●
confidence handling dangerous materials and equipment

FINDING A JOB
There are grants available to help people in some creative areas, and business start-up loans and grants if you want to work for yourself. Your local library will be able to point you toward sources of financial help.

Further Information

BOOKS

Ferguson's Careers in Focus: Design, Ferguson Publishing, 2005.

Battenfield, Jackie. *The Artist's Guide: How to Make a Living Doing What You Love*, Da Capo Press, 2009.

Dunkleberger, Amy. *So You Want to be a Film or TV Editor?*, Enslow, 2008.

Glass, Sherri and Jim Wentzel. *Cool Careers Without College for People Who Love Manga, Comics, and Cartoons,* Rosen Pub Group, 2007.

Hinton, Kerry. *Cool Careers Without College for Music Lovers*, Rosen Pub. Group, 2007.

Horn, Geoffrey M. *Camera Operator*, Gareth Stevens Pub., 2009.

O'Neill, Joseph. *Movie Director*, Cherry Lake Pub, 2010.

WEB SITES

http://www.adigitaldreamer.com
Read career articles, find graphic design schools, & discover jobs. Also explore video game design, animation & photography.

http://www.bookjobs.com
Whoever you are and whatever your interests, you may find a place for yourself in the publishing industry. Learn about the types of publishers, the types of jobs available, and more on this web site.

http://www.bls.gov/oco
For hundreds of different types of jobs in the creative and media field, the Occupational Outlook Handbook gives information on education needed, earnings, job prospects, and more.

http://www.khake.com/page43.html
Explore careers in Broadcast Media and Journalism with links to job descriptions which include information such as daily activities, skill requirements, salary and training required.

http://nasad.arts-accredit.org
NASAD provides information to potential students and parents, consultations, statistical information, professional development; and policy analysis.

Glossary

anechoic made to prevent echoes

articulate able to speak fluently and expressively

commission contract to produce something specific in exchange for payment

copywriter someone who writes the text for commercials, brochures, packaging, and so on

corporate relating to a business

decor interior decoration

dummy a model book made up with blank pages and used to sketch out the text and illustrations of a planned book

foreign rights the right to print and sell a book in a foreign language or country

internship unpaid position working in an organization to gain experience

line-producing managing the budget and day-to-day aspects of film production

mixing desk electronic equipment used to "mix" or process sound for recording or broadcast

package a completed sequence of an interview or recorded story to include in a TV or radio broadcast

pattern cutting cutting paper patterns used to make copies of a garment

picket line a line of protesters or strikers who try to prevent workers or customers from gaining access to a business or site

pitch to try to sell an idea, article, or creative work by outlining the idea behind it and how it will be produced

portfolio a collection of creative work, or records or evidence of work (such as photos of furniture or gardens)

post-production the processing of a film after it has been shot, consisting of editing and adding extras such as special effects and titling

prostheses an artificial body part

prototype an early design of an object

pyrotechnic relating to fire

rough cut the first attempt at a film sequence made by cutting and splicing bits of film or video

runner a general assistant in a film production unit

sourcing finding a source

splicing joining together film sequences

storyboard a sketch of the sequence of an animation or film shown as thumbnails (small pictures) of key frames

sync synchronize (run at the same time)

taxidermy the art of stuffing and preserving dead animals

trim buttons, beads, and other extras that may be added to a costume

typesetter someone who works with type (lettering designs)

Index